Messages
to my
younger self

The Legacy Collection Presents

Messages
to my
younger self

Messages to Nourish
and Heal the Soul
with love from Carnelian Moon

by Eighteen Inspirational Women

Carnelian Moon
PUBLISHING

Published by Carnelian Moon Publishing Inc.
Ottawa, Canada

www.carnelianmoonpublishing.com

Cover design by Jennifer Insignares
Interior design by Simon Brimble
Edited by Judith Richardson Schroeder

Paperback ISBN: 9781989707111
eBook ISNB: 9781989707128

Dedication

This book is dedicated with love to your younger self. The part of you that is ready to receive the inspiring, uplifting messages shared here, the part of you that recognizes that you are ready to seek the much-needed support and encouragement on your journey.

We dedicate this book to your journey so far, to the empowered steps you will be taking as a result and to your journey onwards. May you find whatever you seek in your life right now.

Achnowledgements

Carnelian Moon Publishing would like to take a moment to honor and acknowledge everyone who has played an integral role in birthing this very first book in the Legacy Collection. All the authors who have shared their intimate messages to their younger selves, sharing hope, possibility and inspiration to others. You have shared from your heart and we know that the power of your words will be received with gratitude and love---thank you for sharing a legacy through your words.

We want to thank our extremely gifted and creative Design Team at Carnelian Moon, Simon Brimble, our book layout and design expert and Jennifer Insignares, our magical book cover design expert. You add sparkles to our work and leave us in awe each day. To our very own, Judith Richardson Schroeder for her editing genius, supporting our authors in enhancing their messages to perfection.

To all the authors around the world that are releasing their work into the world daily, your healing journey is witnessed through your words and we are grateful for your inspiration.

To the little children inside of us all---keep believing and keep dreaming.

We are filled with gratitude for you all.

Contents

Introduction

A message is *"a communication in writing, in speech, or by signals."* There are messages all around us that we receive in various forms every day. Some of the messages we receive are based on the past. So, what if you could receive a message from your older self, the part of you that has already lived through a number of experiences and learned extraordinary messages? Imagine receiving a message that would support you in making a life-changing decision?

At some time in your life, you probably uttered the words *"I wish I knew that when I was younger!"* You may have looked at your life wondering what it would be like if only you had known a particular thing at a particular point in time.

The vision of this book came about as a result of a conversation between the two Co-Founders of Carnelian Moon Publishing. They were talking about introducing a special series of books to share lessons learned to a younger generation and future generations, kind of leaving a legacy behind through words. There were so many lessons they were sharing with each other which were so powerful and they both said, *"imagine if we knew that when we were younger?"* From that conversation, the Legacy Collection was born. This is the very first book in the Legacy Collection Series where everyday people, just like you, share their special messages of those intimate details they wished they knew when they were younger that they know would have supported various choices in their own lives.

Each of the authors share their intimate messages that they wished they knew when they were younger to support you in your own journey. These messages cover various areas of life, sharing messages of advice, support, hope, inspiration, empowerment, love, and so much more. This book is one that can be read time and again to receive the message that is needed at that moment in time so be prepared to open the book up and know that the message you read is the message that is needed to support your heart and soul at that time.

As you read through, you will notice that each author has chosen a symbol that represents her journey, her message and her overall being. You will find that some of these messages and symbols connect with you more than others. The book is meant for you to be able to read it time and time again. If you have a day where you are not feeling at your best and you need some encouragement or uplifting, pick the book up, open it up and allow yourself to connect to the chapter that you are guided to. That is the message you are meant to receive on that day.

"I alone cannot change the world, but I can cast a stone across the waters to create many ripples."

-Mother Teresa

This book is a gift from the heart of every author who has shared within these pages to your heart.

Be open to the possibilities as you embrace all that awaits you and know that you are never alone in your journey.

Love from Your Older Self!

Honor the Voice of Your Soul

by Konyka M. Dunson

Dear Younger Self,

Standing on the edge of the river, as the breeze drifted by, I gazed into the sunset, reflecting on what has been and what will be. As the evening sky faded into a glorious memory, I meditated on the power of the moment. Underlying every moment, experience, and every path ventured

-- I had made a decision. Within that decision -- consciously or unconsciously, fearfully or faithfully — I listened to a voice -- a voice that guided my next move -- telling me who to love, what to create next, or whether to pursue a cherished vision. In the stillness, I realized that my power lay in a decision: Whose voice would I listen to? Would I listen to the voice of others, the multitude of doubts, or would I listen to the voice of my soul?

We are inundated with voices. Colleagues, family, friends, social media, and leaders of all kinds offer perspectives to inform or influence every decision. At times, the voices can be helpful. Other times, the voices become a noisy cacophony that drowns out the most important voice —your own. Your innermost voice, flowing from your soul, speaks in power, clarity, and wisdom. Unencumbered by the opinions of others and deeper than even your own thoughts, which at times can be reactive or doubtful, your voice is divine. Yet, it is a voice that you must learn to appreciate, listen to, and honor. The voice of your soul dwells in truth. Your voice, anchored to your soul, the unlimited and eternal part of you, connects you with the Creator and all that is.

Often as women, the concept of honor -- to honor oneself, your own voice, your own soul, may not sound humble or gracious enough for the woman you are expected or supposed to be. Honor is reserved for parents, leaders, and the Almighty God. Yet to honor your own voice is to hear the part of your soul, the glorious God-given voice within you. As you look at your life from a bird's eye view, from God's view, peer deeply into your decisions and ask: Did you honor the voice of your soul?

Looking back on my decisions, at times, I listened to my own voice and felt the joyful flow of triumph. Other times, as the echoes of doubters and naysayers prevailed, letting fear decide, I felt the painful sting of regret. Yet, in extraordinary moments, the voice beckoned me into the unknown, and I decided to trust my own voice and all that would unfold.

The voice of your soul is your blessed compass. To decide to love when it may not make sense. To leap when it is not practical. To say yes, because it feels so right. In your moments of decision, whether small or monumental, be still. Get quiet -- dwell in gratitude for your voice and the Creator that endows it -- and listen. What is the voice of your soul telling you? Honor the voice of your soul. And let her lead the way.

Your Older Self!

Receive Your Raindrops

by Cindy Winsor

Dear Younger Self,

One very ordinary summer day, my family and I went to a BBQ with friends. It was a beautiful day, just like any other summer day; one you might easily take for granted and not think much about. It certainly didn't seem like a day that a most remarkable thing could happen without any of us even realizing it.

After dinner, the sun decided to dip behind the clouds, and as it got darker outside, drop by drop, the rain slowly began to fall. Chantal, a beautiful French woman just learning her way with English, was the first to feel the slight peck of a drop and asked if anyone else had *"received a raindrop."* Of course, we giggled at her choice of words, but she never realized how on that day, her simple broken English sentence would change my perspective about my life.

One by one, each of us held our breath, looking to the sky and waiting with anticipation to receive *our* raindrop. One by one, every grown adult around the table that day felt a drop and was excited to receive it.

I watched in awe as these people, all with busy lives, problems of their own, kids to raise, households to run, illnesses to battle, slowed down for just a few moments, stopped and waited to feel the rain. We waited with excitement as each of us announced we had felt our own special drop, and then we would receive another, and another as the rain increased its rhythm.

Such a beautiful, ordinary day, during a typical rain shower profoundly changed my outlook. The Universe gave me such an incredible gift that day – a window to see into my own life more joyfully.

Lives are so busy, filled with chaos, and the need to adapt to change at a moment's notice. Days are cluttered with housework, homework, jobs, and a million other things, tugging at our sleeves, vying for our time.

The world itself is so full of negativity, sadness, and discord. It doesn't have to be that way, though. I needed to stop back then and be excited again, and ready for what the Universe wanted to give me. I realized the more open I was to receive, and the more I looked instead of just going through the motions, there was so much more to look for every day just waiting for me. I had so much more to receive than I realized.

Since that day, I look at my life completely differently. It doesn't have to be a big momentous thing that happens. The little things are just as vast and full of meaning if I allow them to be. I now recognize those gifts, receiving them humbly, and I am thankful for what I have, big or small. Too often, we take things for granted and put them on the back burner to deal with later. Beauty surrounds us always, but we are often too wrapped up in our own lives to see it. Or to receive it. I realized then, as I understand now, I had to stop. Stop and recognize the gifts I receive every day.

Stopping and enjoying what I have been given each day. I recognize the importance of anticipating the day with eagerness, not dread, about what may be coming next. And lastly, I realized then, as I do now, the need to be gracious for others when they have succeeded. I needed to wait for my raindrop with excitement and anticipation, just as with life, and for the gifts the Universe is ready to give my fellow humans as well. It's not a race; it's not a comparison.

Slow down. Enjoy your life. Look around you to see how blessed you indeed are. Never forget to anticipate and prepare to receive your raindrop.

Your Older Self!

Brilliantly You!

by Debbie Belnavis-Brimble

My Precious Child,

I want to remind you that whatever you are going through right now, wherever you are in your life's journey, YOU ARE a BRILLIANT being!

I hear you screaming, objecting to this statement because your life doesn't reflect this, and you are close to giving up! *"How can I be brilliant when I don't feel brilliant and my life doesn't appear to be brilliant?"* I hear you ask.

There have been many moments in my life when I've been you and I've uttered those same doubtful words. There were times when life felt so bleak, and that may be the same for you, however there has always been hope. Even when I didn't know how things would play out, I reminded myself of my own inner brilliance and I am honored to have the opportunity to prepare you, by reminding you to always have hope by believing in *your* own unique brilliance as well.

For me, your brilliance is like the beautiful and precious diamond that is buried deep within the earth's core until that divine moment in its journey when the volcanic pipes push it closer to the surface. You are that diamond, that precious gem, and there are parts of you yet to be discovered. You have buried your brilliance so deep inside of you, and you protect it so fiercely because it is the most precious possession you have ever owned. It is this unique part of you, similar to your fingerprint. Only you have this exact combination and design.

It includes your purpose, passion, values, courage, confidence, resilience, personality, love and so much more. Your Inner Brilliance is the *diamond of your soul.*

There will be times in your life when you just don't feel connected to yourself fully, you may not want to acknowledge your brilliance. Instead, you will opt for placing others on a pedestal, focusing on *their* dreams, goals, vision and priorities. I've been in that exact place where I gave to others more than I gave to myself. I poured into others as I wanted badly to prove that I was worthy, that I was valuable and that I *added* value.

Please understand there will be times in your life when you feel others are more valuable than you are, they contribute more to society than you do, they are a huge asset to humanity and you might place them on a pedestal, only to be disappointed by them when the truth about them is revealed to you.

Now, it's easy for me to say that, and even accept it as my truth and so too will you. After all, I have lived your lifetime and I have been shown the evidence time and time again as I discover and rediscover who I truly am and in turn, who you truly are. You see my beautiful, you were born with a precious gem deep inside of you, just like a diamond buried deep within the earth's core, being pushed to the surface for others to see its beauty. You too are meant to be seen, heard and experienced. It's time to rediscover, acknowledge, and embrace who you have always been, who you were created to be and who you will always be.

Be boldly brilliant and embrace your unique inner brilliance within you always.

I love you yesterday, today, tomorrow and always my precious!

Your Older Self!

To my Courageous, Adventurous Younger Self

by Sara Olson

Little One,

You are 5, and I am your 45-year-old older self. I want you to know:

Even though your parents fight a lot, it does not mean you aren't seen or not important – it only means that's all they know. They don't know a different way. Your Dad is grieving his father, and your Mom is grieving hers. They don't know how to process it and are taking their grief out on each other and the children.

When your Grandma wants a hug, squeeze a little longer – don't run off so quickly.

When Mom reads you a bedtime story, appreciate her and learn to love and respect her because few have – the sooner you understand this, the sooner you will gain self-respect.

When you are in 8th grade, and Matt wants to kiss you – do it. Keep in touch with your high school friends, Tiffany, Brian, Allison, and Dawn. Visit them, talk with them often, go to their weddings, celebrate their successes, and console them in their losses.

When you are 19, you will have a beautiful little girl. I want you to make sure to spend time with her playing, hugging, and pouring love into her. Help her see how precious she is, and help her learn to stay young longer, don't expect too much of her. She is learning, how to be a powerful woman too.

At the age of 21, you will have a gifted Son, an answered prayer. Spend less time worrying about getting chores done and more time laughing and making memories. Teach him how to read even though you are a tired Single Mom.

You must read a few books by the age of 25, especially the book "Co-dependency no More," which will teach you to break the co-dependency pattern and an essential lesson about establishing boundaries. It's okay to question authority, it's okay to say no, and it's okay not to be so damn nice. Being nice will not earn you friends!

Read the Bible and a pamphlet "How to be Free from Bitterness." It has an important message about forgiveness and gratefulness. Forgiveness will help you let go of your anger. Don't repeat your parents' pattern of anger. Forgive them and forgive yourself; we all make mistakes and grow from them.

In the matter of love, be picky, raise your standards, don't settle, and don't give handouts to those who aren't willing to do the work themselves. Don't force love, if it's meant to be; it will be. You deserve to be happy. Demand respect. Again, don't be so damn nice!

In 2007 you will make a decision that will set a trajectory in motion – whatever you do – don't move to Arizona. Move home to Moscow and keep your children with you.

Let your heart be your compass. Keep smiling; keep the faith. Be spiritual but not religious. Keep learning, growing, and enjoying the sunshine. Don't lose your adventurous free-loving ways.

These things are the core of who you are, and they will help you through many trials. You are brave. You are enough. Will you remember me?

Your Older Self!

A Life Worth Living

by Janet Wiszowaty

Dear Younger Self,

Today I was reminded of my first experience of writing my own obituary while attending a personal development workshop. I had never thought of it as a tool to live my life by. I had actually forgotten about the experience; it took a Memorial Parade to wake me up and make me take a good look at what I am creating in my life.

As I watched the motorcade move through the community I was visiting at the time, honoring the man who was much revered, I began to think of the impact this man had on his community. His life ended too soon due to a careless driver who had hit the motorcycle he was riding. I now think it might be time to do this exercise again and re-evaluate my life; I think it would be a valuable writing exercise to undertake again.

Had I been assigned this exercise in high school; my life might have been a little different. When we are young, we do not think of our demise nor what impact we have on others. Watching this parade and hearing people talk about this man made me wonder about the mark I am leaving behind when I pass from this world. Have I been loving and caring to those around me?

Have I made people smile when they were sad?

I have been blessed to have a family, grandchildren, a great-grandchild and many friends around the world. I tithe to a variety of agencies, but is that enough?

What legacy do I want to leave behind? What do I want people to say about me when I am gone? Every once in a while, an event as powerful as this occurs, and I stop and think of where my life is and what I have accomplished.

Maya Angelou — 'I've learned that people will forget what you said, people will forget what you did, but people will never forget how you made them feel.'

What do you want people to say about you when you are gone? In today's media, there are so many negatives; remember that there are great people that went before us – *Mother Teresa, Nelson Mandela, Martin Luther King Jr., Mohandas Karamchand Gandhi, Winston Churchill* as well as *Wayne Dyer, Louise Hay,* to name a few. Other role models are still with us today; one of my favorites, as well as one of my mentors, is Jack Canfield. If you have ever read a Chicken Soup for the Soul book, you may recognize Jack Canfield as one of the co-authors of Chicken Soup for the Soul, as well as the author of The Success Principles. There are others who are leaving an impression and legacy. All you have to do is look around; I am sure you can find some in your neighborhood, community, or even in your family.

Make a list with two columns, under one column list those who have left a positive impression/feeling with you and under the other column, list one of the people who made. you feel uncomfortable. Take a good look at the lists. Which person do you want to be?

Remember, it never hurts to take a look at your life, and it is always okay to Course Correct.

Your Older Self!

Beyond the Ledge of Fear

by Judith Richardson Schroeder

Oh, My Precious One,

You have had so many exciting journeys in your life! You have always chosen to take the adventure path, true to your Birth sign. You seem to want still to explore that path least traveled.

Many view this personality trait as courageous or

exciting, but some see it as a bit "flighty." They see you as someone who loves to chase shiny objects, who gets bored quickly, or loses interest in projects swiftly.

They tend to view your adventurous flights as "not focused" or lacking in direction. That may very well be true for somethings, but dear one, I want to remind you that you have also achieved many things you might otherwise never have, were it not for your willingness to step beyond the ledge of fear to explore! You have set goal after goal for yourself ever since you were very young. And, you have, through perseverance, manifestation, and actions, achieved everyone!

Some of your goals have taken many years -- like wanting to have a story published in Chicken Soup for the Soul. Remember when you first had that thought? Way back in the 90s when Chicken Soup for the Soul stories first came to market! I recall your putting that goal out to the Universe. Emphasizing it with the phrase, "Someday I will...." And, someday, you did! You finally decided to send a story in for a book being published in September 2017, and you were successfully published in that book! You chose to tell your story of a dream you had about your father years earlier, who had just passed away. Your someday took time to arrive as you put it on a back burner to achieve other things first, but it DID come, and it was a day of celebration that you took deeply to heart.

There have been many such goals set and achieved over the years; recounting them would be a lengthy list! Yet, you still have moments of doubt. Doubt that you are worthy of achievement. Doubt that you are worthy of success. Doubt that you are as excellent as those around you!

So, dear one, this is my wish for you. I wish for you to cast aside those doubts. All of them. Every last one. For, as of right now, you are and always have been someone who has achieved so much!

You are blessed with an uncanny inner knowing, a sense for what is meant to be and of how it is meant to unfold for you.

You are a Life Experi-Mentor! And, for that, you have a zest for the unknown, and of the possibilities that might result! Your explorations in this vein have taken you and will continue to take you to places you know divinely are meant for you to explore.

Never lose that wonderfully adventurous spirit, dear heart!

Always remain your wonderfully explorative, adventurous, and free to be you self! That is what I love MOST about you, and that is what the world needs more of because it is those beautiful qualities that have always helped you step beyond the ledge of fear and explore the world that lies outside your comfort zone with more ease than most! Please continue to do more of this, for it is who you are and just one of many things you do BEST!

Your Older Self!

Do It Through Fear

by Carra Dixon

Dear Younger Me,

What is fear? By definition: fear is to be afraid, (of something or someone), as likely to be dangerous, painful, or threatening. Now, let's also make up our own definitions and acronyms for this powerful word: **F**alse **E**vidence **A**ppearing **R**eal. **F**orget **E**verything **A**nd **R**un, or **F**ace **E**verything

And Rise.

Fear is fake, A phony! It is also meant to test your ability to be great. Fear can debilitate you at times. Fear can start a downward spiral of negative thoughts and feelings. Fear can stop you from achieving goals or making new friends. Fear can change your life in a split second!

What if fear wasn't a factor? *What if* you did what you wanted and left fear right where it stands? *What if* we could do the things we desire despite the fear?

While I take time to realize why I am where I am in my life today, I can certainly take the time to sit here and blame it on fear. I can make many excuses and I can also feel badly for the choices I've made. I have had so many dreams that I chose to pass over or run away from.

All because I allowed fear to dictate my life and my choices.

We've all wondered about the *what ifs,* haven't we? *What If* I did apply for that job and didn't fear being under qualified? I could be at the top of the company today, and all the under-qualified fears would be out the window. Or *what if I was* denied the job and as a result found something better suited to me elsewhere? Either way, I did not get harmed or fatally impacted by the experience! No matter the outcome, good did come from it in the form of a valuable lesson learned.

I will have grown through the experience because I did it *through* fear. I think the biggest fear there is, is not knowing what is ahead. But our failure comes from not even attempting to try to find out where that experience might lead to.

At some point in life, you have to decide to say F fear! Excuse the language, but overpowering the fear gives you confidence and gives your power back to YOU. If it is not directly affecting your health or well-being, and it isn't a threat to your life, be aware of the fear but do it anyway! I hope you don't think these big-time celebrities or people of higher power didn't experience their own fear or never experienced it on a day by day basis, because *that* is not true. If you genuinely believe it. If you speak it into existence and are patient through the fear, your best outcome from the experience *will* happen. If it is meant to be, it will be, but you have to be willing to go after it. You have to keep your dreams at the forefront of your belief and just step forward and go after it!

Do it through fear, no matter how challenging you may feel it is.

The worst that can happen is that you will receive a *NO*. Well, that wasn't meant to be! So, now, what lesson did you learn from this? What can you do to improve your situation? Your perception of the situation should have a positive outlook no matter how devastated you are by the outcome. Don't fail by not trying or by choosing to give up. Instead, move on to the next opportunity. That *NO* you just received should give you a sense of comfort. That *NO* should not and will not break you. It is just one NO in the line of many possibilities to reach a YES! So, step forward and do it through the fear!!!

Your Older Self!

The Evolution of Me

by Jean Day

My Dear Young One,

The life you will live will have so many curves, twists and turns, Jean. I stand here now forty-six years old with an abundance of experiences to reflect upon and share with you in this message. There have been many achievements, a few losses and some unexpected victories, but as I look back now, I want you to know the journey ahead of you, but most importantly, the strength within you!

You are such a wild child full of anger, fear and feistiness. It is fear that will affect your life the most. You will grow up in a home with domestic violence that continues even after your parents' divorce. You won't know just how deeply this will impact your life, or how it will shape you, but you will come through it all despite the challenges.

No, my dear young Jean you won't be able to protect your mother from pain and hurt, though you will take on that role many times throughout your life.

You will also love your father but fear him. He has never so much as spanked you, but you will always fear his strong presence.

You will always remember that your mom did the best she could, but her bouts of major depression have forced you to grow up so quickly.

Your incredible shyness around people will come from your belief that you don't see anything special about yourself. But you will befriend a teacher in high school, and she will exemplify all that you wish to be -- beautiful, confident, fun and Hollywood-like! Your bond with her will be a special one.

You will move to LA!!! Your life will change in many ways! College, what a blast you will end up having!

Mom will come live with you as she continues fighting her demons. Her fight and those demons will follow her till the end of her life. As an adult you can't imagine that you will also develop a mental illness. There will be such a time of darkness for you as you also fight demons like you could never imagine. But, through these struggles you will also experience hope and belief in who you are becoming!

You will discover the gift that becoming a Nichiren Buddhist gives you, and you will credit it for saving your life!

Your biggest fear will happen on September 3rd, 2010. You will find mom gasping for air in the apartment you share with her at 6:15 a.m. that day, and from then on, your life will forever be changed. You will miss mom deeply and forever. But you will always remember and love her.

You will regret not having children of your own, but you will choose to live on your own again, all while you battle and overcome the demon of mental illness and while successfully teaching college.

You will, in spite of your struggles, manifest all of the dreams you envision for your career and its success.

Jean, you are going to go into your forties and still be single. There will really be no special man during this time, and you will feel times of great loneliness. But you will trust in yourself and in what is to be for you.

The fear you have of driving will continue to haunt you, and you will choose not to get your driver's license because of it. That will remain the battle of a lifetime that you will still be fighting at the age of forty-six. But it is a decision you feel is the right one for you.

It will be hard for you and your dad at times to

understand each other, but you will forgive your parents for the difficult times they put you through when younger, and the journey to understanding will develop as it is able to.

In your forties, you will become a mentor to a 5-year old little girl and that will allow you to lavish all the affection you have in your heart on her. She will bring you so much joy!

But, through it all dear Jean, all of the challenges you will face will make you stronger. I just want you to remember…that you have overcome things that many people might find too difficult to face. You can achieve anything you put your mind to! You are an amazing woman Jean; you MUST remind yourself of this, especially when there is no one else there to remind you.

Deep inside you is the lion and the lion will always win. I will always love you, dear Jean.

Love,

Your Older Self!

Love Thy Self

by Chrisa Riviello

Dear Younger Self,

Self-love is so important. The greatest love of all that should be taught very early on in life is to love yourself. In the past, I put limitations on myself when it came to love.

I didn't have the "model" to teach me about love

and relationships. I was taught about fear, pain, and how to feel alone.

I surrounded myself with the wrong people. I became a people pleaser in order to be liked by others. In relationships, I kept quiet and did as I was told and did not fight for my rights or my opinion in any matter. I would go with the flow with no voice of my own.

Even in my years in education, I was never taught how important it was to love yourself. However, what I did learn is that we are the product of the environment in which we grow up. And, many of us have our definition of love because of that environment. And in turn, it leaves many of us unable to understand how to love or be loved.

When my marriage was headed for divorce, I knew that something had to change within me. I mustered up the courage to get out of a bad situation that had me broken and scarred at the time.

I had to heal and learn to love myself in spite of the previous negative qualities pointed out to me that made me feel undesirable. So, my journey of self-love and healing began.

People can only change if they want to, and only if they realize their way is not creating a loving environment but only creating a negative one. My experience allowed me to decide to love myself, heal myself, and understand life all around me. Since then, I have taken steps to be my authentic self and to share my loving light that now shines for all to see.

The only true love I have felt this far has been from my children. It is an unconditional love that gives you the courage and strength to be better. I had to better myself to be able to teach them the life lessons that are important in any relationship. You have to learn to love and be happy with yourself before you can do so with others. Kids need to model after someone happy, strong, and healed within themselves.

What would I tell my younger self? Well, first, I am here to teach and guide you to a life that allows you to choose love. To be yourself and be comfortable with yourself. To find your passion and let *that* be your life's purpose. To do what you love and be happy, because then the universe will provide. For myself and my family, I have created this loving, supportive environment. So please know that it is ok, no matter what you may have gone through in your life. It will make you stronger as it has made me the stronger woman I am today. Key words to live by -- Love Thy Self.

Your Older Self!

Quit Comparing Yourself to Others

by Allistar Banks

Dear Younger Me,

Let me just say this about who you are from the inside out. You are enough! And, so I say to you lovingly, stop complaining about where you are in life versus where others.

Comparing yourself to others leads to a never-ending path of unhappiness. That unhappiness will eventually spiral into jealousy, inadequacy, and inferiority. It will cause you unnecessary stress, unwanted anxiety, depression, and so much more. You will exhaust yourself trying to accomplish what others have accomplished. Don't be concerned, the universe will supply your needs. Pray and have faith, and everything will fall into place. You are enough just the way you are, and you are exactly where you need to be in your life.

Observing how others look, feel, what their job title is, their social status, the kind of house and car they own, the clothes they wear on their back will only serve to make you feel insecure and unworthy while a part of their social circle. My dear, you are so much more than material things. You are a ray of light and beauty that can't be replaced. You are one-of-a-kind simply by the way you talk, look, smile, show-up, and by the gifts and talents you possess. Just remember that you are worthy and uniquely you.

Embrace your inner and outer beauty. Allow that big heart of yours to open up and show the world how you warmly help and heal others. Allow your appearance to radiate and light up every room you enter. You are so worth it.

Your inner beauty represents the heart of gold pumping within you. The heart of gold that radiates healing, helping others, spreading kindness, and putting a smile on someone else's face. The heart that can hear a thousand tears. Your heart can heal others through words of affirmations. Just let those affirmations pour out of you and express them to the world. Your inner beauty is so wonderful and precious my dear.

Your outer beauty is your physical appearance. The way you take such good care of yourself lets others know that you care about the body God has given you. Your outer beauty represents the great smile, face, eyes, ears, and nose that are yours. By eating healthy, exercising, and getting enough rest you faithfully rejuvenate your body. Your whole being makes you beautifully different from everyone else.

I would love to hear you say, "I do not need to be like everyone else. I am enough just the way I am. The way I am separates me from the crowd. My eyes, face, smile, and the way I carry myself is beautiful. My job and love life and social status are not all who I am as a person. I am a unique child of God. God says, "you are valuable, new, you have my spirit, you are transformed through Me, and you represent Me." Remember, I am good enough just the way I am."

No longer compare yourself to others because . . .
- You are enough.
- You are a ray of light.
- You are worthy.
- You are one-of-a-kind.
- Your gifts and talents matter.

Sincerely,

Older Me!

LET GO!

by Cathy Gagliardi

My Love,

As I look at the youth of today, I see such beautiful, bright beams of light. With worldly knowledge and overwhelming compassion comes a weight of worry and concern for their future. Such conflicting messages such as, "Be carefree and enjoy your youth. Your job is to experience life and have fun." And then..." Change the world! You are the future! You are responsible for our elders. You need a money-driven career to succeed!" And then those words are so easily tossed away by saying, "So get out there and do your thing!"

Young Cathy was carefree.

I picture myself on a blanket in a meadow under the bluest of skies. My message to young Cathy would go something like this:

Our earth is a beautiful place to be, and your glowing spirit is here to brighten it just by being you.

How you see the world may be unique in the eyes of those around you. The innocent, cutesy names people refer to you as, like flighty, bubbles, butterfly, have been right on. Even though you find it hard to keep your feet on the ground, remember how intelligent, strong, and dedicated you are. Being a dedicated worker is important; you will find it stimulates you to achieve even more in your life.

My message to you, my wide-eyed adventurer, is

to "Let Go." Give yourself permission to breathe in the magical air and breathe out those emotional restraints. Listen to both sides of your brain, the logical one as well as the spiritual one.

Let yourself seep into the vibrations of the earth. Hear your intuitive voices without judgment and doubt. In the precious moments when something humorously catches you by surprise, I invite you to let go and laugh until your belly hurts. Remember, it is okay to be spontaneous and not always take the safe route.

Let go of the fear that you may hurt someone if you do what is best for yourself. Embrace the love you feel. It is a gift. As you feel the deep love you have for everything, just let it flow and relax. The overwhelming desire to save the planet full of beautiful children, individuals, and animals is a lovely thought but not productive when it debilitates you.

Spread your love every day. That's what you can do.

Letting go, by the way, is just another term used to describe opening up to experiences. Vulnerability is not only being transparent but feeling safe enough to let your guard down and speak your truth or show your passion in whatever you love. It is where miracles happen. The joy is memorable and addictive when you can Let Go. The words spoken can reveal messages hidden deep inside that will release barriers and promote clarity and actions from the heart.

So, my flighty, bubbly little butterfly, get ready for the opportunities that will help you live your truth. You already love with your whole heart, now Let Go and experience with your entire being!

Your Older Self!

Food Will Not Solve Your Problems

by Allistar Banks

Dear Younger Me,

I am sorry for how I used food to comfort you and soothe your feelings and emotions through life. Food is not supposed to soothe away your troubles, pains, negativity; but instead should help you stay active and enjoy vitality and good health. A lifestyle built upon proper nutrition, self-reflection, exercise, healthy relationships, meditation, and prayer is a good life.

With proper nutrition comes understanding portion control and choosing healthy foods to fuel your body. Using a dietary guideline will help you with proper portion measurements helping you understand how many servings of fruits, vegetables, whole grains, fats, and other wholesome foods you need. Eating healthy doesn't have to be hard or time-consuming, it just takes learning the basics of portion control.

Self-reflection requires journaling, praying, and meditating and provides ways to release the troubles in your personal life and at school. Journaling helps release you from the worries and concerns of the day. Praying helps to center your life through God. Meditating clears the brain fog from your mind to help you think more clearly.

By practicing proper nutrition, self-reflection, exercise, praying, and meditating, you can achieve mindful eating and succeed in thinking less about food. By recognizing and understanding your food triggers, you can be on the path of success while developing a healthy lifestyle. Exercising helps to release happy endorphins and burn fat and tone up your body. Praying allows you to give all of your cares to God. Meditating can help calm the chatter in your mind to allow for focus and to help you look and feel your best from the inside out.

Lastly, I want to give you a hug and kiss and tell you just how much I love you from the inside out.

Life wasn't easy while going through puberty, or while your mom was part of the dating scene after her divorce. Or while managing your brother's fragile x syndrome or trying to make new friends at a new school. It wasn't easy while facing peer pressure and hoping to fit in.

I know that food was your safe haven to run to when you didn't want to face your problems at home and school but know that food is not the way out of a problem. Food does not take away puberty, your mom's trials or challenges in finding a good man. It doesn't make your brother's disorder better, and it doesn't make peer pressure or fitting in any easier. You have so much to offer to the world because of your abundance of kindness and compassion.

The final words of advice I want to share about eating right comes from something grandad always said, "If it doesn't grow from the dirt, do not eat it." He knew locally grown produce doesn't have any added colors, preservatives, or fillers. It tastes fresh and not artificial. Before you grab that Little Debbie cake or bag of chips, keep granddaddy's wise words in mind, "If it doesn't grow from the dirt, do not eat it." Sugar and salt are only a temporary high to make you feel better in the moment. Feeling good from the inside out requires all of these special and well-balanced ingredients to help you enjoy a long-lasting healthy lifestyle for years to come.

Sincerely,

Older Me!

US

by Cindy Winsor

Sweet Little One,

Oh, my sweet self... if only I could go back and talk to you, make you listen, make you see. What amount of hurt I might have prevented if only you were taught a few basic things. If only you saw yourself the way I remember you now, that feeling you had when you looked in the mirror would be so incredibly different. You are vibrant. Funny. Kind and loyal. You are so brilliant, and you have such an incredible heart. Your passion is your greatest asset, not your only weakness.

Abandonment.

Even the word itself is enough to send the feeling of terror through your veins. Nobody wants to be abandoned, but for you -- for us, it's so much worse. It's a fundamental fear that we struggle to deal with every single day. We try to avoid it at all costs, and yet, oddly enough, it's the one thing that happens to us the most often. Dad, brother, husband. All to leave you, moving on, and forgetting your very existence. Oddly, you're not the common denominator. Well, you *are*, but not in the way you believe. What took me a very long time to realize is this - what if instead of being terrified of abandonment, we made sure we never felt abandoned again?

You've spent so long attempting to keep peace, to ignore hurts, to put your needs on the backburner, all so you won't be left behind... yet by doing so, you are ignoring and treating the one person who *won't* leave, who *can't* leave, so poorly that you loathe everything about her!

I'm talking about you, my sweet self. About us! *We* are the one person who will be with us, guaranteed, for our **ENTIRE** life. We won't leave you! We **cannot** leave you! She is me, and we are her. Why are we treating her like she doesn't exist? Like she doesn't matter? She is the most important person in your life, yet you forget her at every turn, and you resent her existence. Why? What has she done to you to make you hate her so?

You are vibrant. So is she!

You are funny and kind and loyal. You must say that often and mean it. Hear it. Believe it.

Here is the excellent news, my sweet self. **YOU CAN CHANGE HER.** You can mold her into everything and anything we desire to be. She is our best friend, our teacher, our healer, and our soul. You can take anything you don't like about her and turn her into what you do like. You can fine-tune her into the best person we have ever met, into the best friend we have ever had. You can teach her to mend her hurts, to soothe her soul.

You can save her from so much hurt, so much pain and torment, if you -- *Just. Put. Her. First.* You have that power to change her and make sure abandonment isn't our most feared word. You don't need someone else to complete us, to save us. You happen to be our Hero. Forever!

Your Older Self!

Life happens for you! I love you!

by Cassie Ferrer

Dear Younger Self,

When I was fifteen through seventeen, my life was an absolute mess! I felt hopeless and entirely out of control. At the time, I would never have guessed I would later start an organization helping women and being a selfless leader who spearheaded an incredible movement!

Looking back now however, this is the letter I would like to write to you, my younger self.

Everything will be ok. Life happens for you, not to you.

Although it may seem like the world is crumbling around you, you will grow from all the events you have experienced, and you will become stronger as you emerge from the other side.

It may appear that your father left you and did not care about you. You may even think that he didn't love you. Those thoughts are your own assumptions and perceptions. I'm confident that he does love you, but maybe he did not make the right choices in his *own* life. It's vital that you love yourself first.

It may seem that your mother decided to send you to the U.S. to get rid of her *own* problems. She made the best decision she could at the time. She may not have *always* made the best decisions at times, but she did the best she could with the resources she had at the time. Please do not get upset with her. Forgive her and set yourself free.

There were dark moments at times, as you went through periods of trauma. Never forget to nurture yourself and be kind to yourself, though.

Some people have wronged you, but you have also met kind individuals that have helped you along the way. You *will* learn to trust again.

It's ok to look inward and listen to your emotions. It would be best if you allowed yourself to feel your emotions. It's ok to be sad and disappointed at certain times. There is no need to mask your emotions for anyone.

There were times that you thought you had been silenced or that your opinions didn't matter. You will continue to learn to speak up and live from your truth.

You have made some bad decisions. Forgive yourself. Take responsibility, but know that you were misguided at the time, and you did not have the role models you needed to guide you toward the right path. In the future, you will meet many positive, strong leaders who will lift you and shape your leadership.

You are beautiful the way you are, inside and out. I know you felt insecure about the way you look, but you will meet many people who appreciate your inner *and* outer beauties.

You may feel that you could not trust or love anyone or that you could not have a family because you did not come from a perfect family yourself. You will learn to love and experience true love.

Do not be embarrassed or feel ashamed about your past. Your past shapes the person you will become. You don't live in the past. You live in the present and you must look for ways to better your future.

The events that happened in the past will allow you to share your story, which will help inspire someone who may be going through a similar journey.

Don't give up on your dreams! Listen to your intuition. You are somebody, and you are significant.

Your Older Self!

P.S. I love you!

The Freedom in Losing it All

by Donna Brown

Dearest One,

This message is for you, my dear one, when you have had to start over, had to walk away from your life as you've known it. It's for you as you lie in bed at night, wondering how much longer you can hold on, and it's for those times when you imagine your escape.

This message shares the courage, strength, love, and joy from the warrior in me to the warrior in you. From my inner child, dancing in a field of wildflowers to your inner child, weaving a daisy chain for her head.

You can do this. You are more resilient than you know. You can rise from the ashes of a life that does not fit your soul to create a new one that may not look like anything you ever imagined, but it will be one you love.

For years I dreamed of the day I would be able to leave. I had always imagined I would be able to bring with me some part of the things I had worked so hard to create. But that is not how things were meant to be. I left with very little, and after a strenuous battle, I almost didn't survive.

I am still not free to speak the story's truth that marked the end of my family as I knew it. A battle that took a toll on my mental, physical and financial health from which I have yet to recover.

I don't think I have ever cried as much in my life as I did the night my son and daughter dropped me off at the place, I have called home for the last few years. Far away from anything I had known, full of someone else's belongings. Not home, but a refuge, nonetheless. I was so grateful just to be there.

I learned so much during my time in that flat with odd furnishings and a lumpy mattress.

I learned I could put myself last, even though I was living on my own. I pushed when I should have rested.

I tried so many things that I thought would make things better, but they made a recovery longer and harder.

I want you to know that you will be ok. You are more resilient than you think.

Be kind to yourself. Listen to your body. Spend as much time as you can resting and recovering. Be ruthless about spending time only with people who support you and only doing things that bring you peace or joy.

Make your decisions from a place of joy and excitement rather than from a place of fear. I promise you it will happen if you let it. Find joy in small things.

Dream big, fat, juicy dreams. Write them down. Draw pictures and sing songs about them. Find out who you want to be. Trust yourself.

In the aftermath of loss, my son said this to me. *"Just think. Now you can do anything you want."*

I know you can too.

Your Older Self!

Focus on What You Can Control

by Cathy Gagliardi

My Love,

My message to my younger self is to look around and see everything and everybody that cannot be controlled directly by you.

From 100% of every situation, what percentage can you currently control?

The likely answer is, *you* can only control YOU!

That's all! That is it, and *that* is very powerful.

I have tried to make my life better by changing others, but now I realize I was the one who needed to change. There is no amount of energy you can spend that will fix others or only control them. They may be influenced by your actions -- perhaps. But, as we wish our actions could become an example that others learn from, we also know that we tend to copy and learn from both the good and bad habits of ourselves and of others, and that tends to follow us from birth. As we experience life, we can choose the best practices that we discover are available to us.

We can choose how we react to a situation, which will make all the difference in the world.

I am still learning every day that my interpretation of the events around me can make me angry, and it is my assumption of what others are implying that can make me feel as though I should feel hurt.

You *can* control these feelings though, by remembering what people say, and how they say it and realizing it comes from their internal story, their personal feelings, and their own expectations of themselves.

Worrying about others and what may have happened, or what might happen could end up feeling debilitating. If that feeling of not having control over something consumes you, take comfort in knowing you can take a slow, deep breath and then ask yourself, "What can I do right now?" The answer may be, "Nothing, in this case." But there is always something that can take the pressure off. I personally like to get in the kitchen and bake or become involved in a great book or a movie.

With every situation, the outcome is affected by what is just beyond my control. What can I affect by my influence, and what can I achieve totally on my own? Sometimes, what has to be done is hard to identify with and can cause extreme guilt within us. I have learned that the answer to guilt is to take action and have patience. I have not yet mastered patience, but if you start to practice now, I promise, you will benefit from this virtue.

You can take comfort in knowing that even overwhelming loneliness is able to be controlled. Reaching out is not a weakness, but a necessity to assist you to work through challenging situations. As humans, we are very social, and we gain many assets & lessons as we create our communities. Each person you have chosen to be in your circle has something to offer, and *you* are definitely valuable.

Love and respect for myself and others have been beautiful gifts and cherished, valuable education to me as I've aged. I can control my thoughts and feelings by remembering to respect others' opinions and their lives, while continuing to take pride in my points of view and in my personal accomplishments.

Never forget. You are in control of your beautiful life!

Your Older Self!

Living your Purpose in the Now

by Mary Ananda Shakti

My Gorgeous Girl,

If there were something I could say to you precious one, most of all it would be to smile and laugh more. Those times when you felt the whole world was against you, well, it wasn't. A lot of it was that you were sensitive when you were being told off or shouted at. When you were shocked, when you felt unloved and uncared for. But you were always loved.

That happened many times in your life when others didn't show their love for you, but you were always loved at a deep level by other loved ones. Hugs for you when you felt disconnected from yourself and others, for when you thought you had to protect yourself from those around you. Hugs for when you cried so hard you thought you would never stop, or feeling you would die from sadness; hugs for you for being resilient and rising from the ashes, for being strong and never failing to love even when you felt unloved.

Mary, you are amazing! You survived a severe car accident to go on to turn your life around to help and support others. You live your authentic self and your truth every day. You qualify your words by living in awareness and being sensitive to others' needs.

You were searching for the meaning of your life, and you discovered it slowly and meaningfully when in the depths of depression, as you searched for the answers. In the beginning, it was from those who walked the path before you, and then some years later, when you had done many trainings and healings, you awoke the fountain of bliss within. It poured from your veins as your heart radiated the purest love. The vibrations of love poured out to every living being you encountered.

You met with the Masters and sat at their tables in your sleeping state. From there, you were no longer a slave to your emotions or everyone else's; Your chattering mind became still and quiet. Your creativity soared as you explored art, soap, and cosmetic making. You made gorgeous hats in their plenty that adorned many a beautiful face. You have a magnificent soul of dazzling bright light that loves to dance.

You are free to roam the universe with full awareness of its beauty. The universe took care of you as you walked in the presence of compassion and love whilst staying present in the moment and by living from your truth.

There were some tough times when closure had to come for some situations, but through it all, you lived in the moment and followed the energy of love, which continues to gracefully take you on your journey.

Dear Mary, relax. Don't worry or be concerned with either past or future. Your power is here in the present, in the now. It is here that you are supreme; this is where you are manifesting all that is — this is where you are making your memories. Always.

Your Older Self!

The Path to Self-Fulfilment and Self-Awareness

by Carra Dixon

Dear Younger Me,

I have realized that two things in my adult life are important in any situation: self-awareness and self-fulfillment.

By definition, self-awareness is the conscious

knowledge of one's character, feelings, motives, and desires. Self-fulfillment is the ability to be satisfied by self without external stimulation, pleasure, or influence. These two characteristics can and will help you go a long way in life. They make relationships better, or for lack thereof, at least run more smoothly through life. They diminish the feeling of loneliness and self-doubt. Overall, self-awareness is to recognize. Self-fulfillment is to accept.

Many people find self-awareness hard because you have to admit things about yourself, which you may not want to. You have to come to terms with the "you" you try to avoid or push away daily. That "negative" side of you that you despise in other people around you. Have you ever looked at someone who is angry and thought, "He/she is always mad or has something mean to say?" When you have a bad day or are just experiencing negativity, can you realize in the moment how it makes you feel? No? Usually that is because you do not accept that side of you and perhaps you wish it didn't exist. That may be a good or a bad thing. The "negative" things you feel about yourself are not necessarily bad because it makes you who you are. We all have similar thoughts and emotions at times. It just depends on how you respond to them and how you deal with them.

So, before you get down or criticize yourself, you must realize these are normal emotions that do not have to change who you are or what you stand for. You are a mix of the good and the bad, not just *one* or the *other*.

Self-fulfillment takes a little more leg work than self-awareness. You don't just think about being self-fulfilled and suddenly feel completely satisfied. You have to know what you want and need in life and then put action behind it. For example, I have a passion for writing. It helps with my depression, loneliness, insecurities, etc. To have a keyboard or pen and paper in front of me brings me a sense of peace and joy that I cannot begin to explain. Your passion, hobbies, or career are things you can healthily use to fulfill your self-fulfillment. Unless you feel dependent on these things in the sense of not knowing what to do without them, if you cannot have access to them, they should work for you.

I believe self-fulfillment allows you to thrive in the present moment. Having things that interest you temporarily fulfills you, but if you cannot sit with yourself --- and only yourself, you should step back and become aware of why this appears to be a problem. I realized I didn't like to be alone because I chose to look to others for my happiness. I wanted to make others happy and feel complete because I myself did not feel complete.

To sum things up, recognize those parts of yourself you *fear* and learn to accept them. Be kind to yourself and know that the feelings, emotions, and problems you have, we all must deal with at some point in our lives. Learn to create your peace and joy without depending upon outside influences. Trust me when I say your relationships, mental health, and career will improve as long as you accept who you are and choose to embrace your purpose here on this earth.

Your Older Self!

Reflections of Self

by Tanisha Chambers

Dear Younger Self,

I love you and everything about you. Your consistent growth and change are what I hold on to. For years many people stated you would one day fall off your high horse. How dare them say that to you, and I thank you for forgiving them and knowing that the only one you can control is you and your actions. Thank you for not allowing the naysayers to hold a place in your mind and disrupt your positive energy. From such a young age, you have carried yourself with respect, love, confidence, and determination. Even though you did not always have confidence and struggled with being mature and being a kid and having fun, you found balance in your life from a young age. I am proud that through all of your transitional years from kid to teenager to young adult and now, as I would say full-blown adulthood, your paradigms have shifted, and you continue to learn new things and unlearn old, non-serving habits.

Your journey is an amazing one. You have sacrificed a lot and never once complained nor let depression stand in the way of your goals and being the star that you were meant to be. You never allowed the people who have wronged you to stop you or block the blessings you were meant to receive. Younger you, if I had the chance to do it over, I would still choose you, for you are the epitome of a genuinely good person. You have always taken care of your family, and nothing you have done has gone unnoticed. Not everything you do will receive recognition; however, that is ok because you have always known what you have brought to the table and never expected anything. So, thank you, little you, for being one of a kind and embarking on this journey with me called life.

Little you always remember; you did everything right. I forgive you for the things you think you should have done differently. We are all human; no one is perfect. So, little you let go and know that you will always be aware of where you have come from. Little you, as you've grown, continue to feel your vulnerability. Know that feeling all of your emotions from the good to the bad is ok. Just as long as you continue to grow and learn all that this world has in store to show and teach you. Continue to break generational history and make a difference that will one day benefit your grandchildren and great-grandchildren. Little you, thank you for being the change that you wanted to see and for noticing and being aware that you need to do something different. Dear self, as I close, I would tell you to continue to show up and "remember that God gives His toughest battles to His strongest soldiers," and you have been deemed strong and worthy!

Love always,

Tanisha

Your Older Self!

The Blessing in Looking Back

by Nikita McKenzie

My Dear Younger Self,

I became a mother two months before my 16th birthday, and I thought I knew everything. I was in a relationship with someone and was exposed to family life I was not familiar with. It was like an escape for me, and in my mind, I believed it would last forever. As deeply in love as I thought

I was, I had no idea what love really was. Nor did I realize this relationship was just a temporary fix for a longing that I didn't know existed and didn't know quite how to put into words. So, I spent my teen and early adult years with someone who loved me their way and made me feel inadequate at the same time. I was so unsure of myself; I had no idea who I was. So, I allowed this relationship to define me.

It took some time, but through this relationship, I experienced the biggest heartbreak of my life. Don't get me wrong. Some of the pain I experienced was self-inflicted. When the time came for me to choose me, I didn't. I couldn't find my courage. I questioned my self-worth. I didn't feel I was even enough for me.

However, God chose to use that to grow me. Looking back, I now realize that it was about so much more than I could even comprehend at the time. I was being cultivated. God was preparing me for my birthing season. I had to be broken so that I could finally discover me. So, as painful as it was, it was necessary. My pain had a purpose!

If I don't now know anything else, I *do* know that I am who I am because of the growth God delivered to me. Although it was a difficult thing that happened to me, I don't take it personally, and I can tell you now it was all part of a much bigger plan. It is about seeing how far I have come that allows me to confidently say to you; *I Am Enough! We are enough!* It is because of what I have overcome that I am empowered now to choose me over and over again. Knowing that my daughter also survived the process and being able to watch her evolve helps strengthen me more as I walk in purpose.

So, my message to you, dear younger self, is simple. Choose you over everything else, and that means choosing those who also choose you. And, don't be afraid to look in the rear-view mirror while doing so. Don't consider stepping backward, but instead, always look to move forward in life. Here's the thing! To reach your destiny, you have to know your starting point. You cannot move from where you are until **YOU** *know where you are and who* **YOU** *are. You are who* **YOU** *say you are when you arrive where you are meant to be. Remember, others already know you. They are just waiting for you to figure it out for yourself. If you are* going to walk in purpose, it will have to be on purpose.

You've got this!

Your Older Self!

Love the Brilliance Around You

by Debbie Belnavis-Brimble

My Precious Child,

I look around every day, and I am reminded of all the brilliance around us, including you. The light that I see in myself, I see in you. I look around in nature and appreciate the beauty everywhere. The beauty I see in you. I invite you to look around you right now. What do you see? Then, go and look in the mirror and ask yourself, *"what beauty have I shared with the world lately?"*

You have a gift so special inside you that it is meant to be shared with the world, and we are all waiting to see you shine brighter than ever before. There *will* be times in your life when you will feel like you have to dim your inner light to make others feel comfortable. My precious, you were never meant to hide in the background. You were not meant to be unseen, unheard, and unfelt.

Every time you change your dreams' direction, make your vision smaller, or choose the more comfortable option, you dim your light. Every time you lessen your light, it's like a star in the night sky has been switched off. Imagine having the night sky without any stars, ever? Isn't it beautiful when you look up, and you see all the beauty on display, one sparkle at a time? Just as beautiful as that display is, you are just as beautiful when you allow your light to shine for others to witness.

There have been times in my life where I settled for less than I desired and, actually, less than I rightly deserved. When I talk about settling, I am talking about *"the act of giving up someone you love or something you value for less than desired. The act of not being able to satisfy your need or want and choosing someone or something of lower standard or value."* I've settled in my own life in many different ways. For example, staying in a relationship because I didn't want the hassle of a messy breakup, which led to my sacrificing finding my soulmate and starting a family earlier. I also settled in a job that I realized wasn't for me, sacrificing my wellbeing due to the stresses of being overworked and undervalued and even being bullied. I could share many instances when I chose to settle for less, rather than claiming my brilliance and soaring in my success. What about you? What are some of the ways you have settled for less in your life?

You now have an opportunity for you to acknowledge that you have settled and readjust your life. I don't regret any of those occasions where I decided to accept less because it allowed me to identify what I really wanted in life and to realize what my heart and soul truly desired. Live your life by always connecting with your inner brilliance. Live your life by connecting with your true desires and remember to shine brightly, embracing your brilliance always. You are brilliant, my precious one.

Always remember, I love you!

Love from Your Older Self! x

Spread Your Wings and Fly

by Janet Wiszowaty

Dear Younger Self,

I want to share an important insight with you that I have learned along the way. It begins with a song, "I've Never Been to Me," sung by a singer, Charlene.

When I first heard this song in the early 1980's

I cried -- not because I had lived the life of the person in the story whom the lyrics spoke of; but because I was unhappy with who I believed I was at the time and always would be.

A high school dropout -- not very smart, or so I had been told many times by my teachers, as well as family members.

I was a good person. I followed the rules and did what was expected of me and did not rock the boat. I did what I thought others wanted me to do and worked hard to please others.

I was a good wife and a so-so mother. I had wanted to be that perfect mother who stayed home with her children and kept a clean house, and always cooked good healthy meals. Believe me, I was not, nor would I ever be that mother. Nine months after my son was born, my old job called me and asked if I could come in for one day and help them out. I came home that night and told my husband I was going to return to work again. I found I was a much better mother when I was working, even if only part-time as I was due to have my second baby in just two months.

Working part-time brought its unique challenges... yes, you guessed it, childcare.

Over the years, I gave up my job several times to stay home with my children and looked after other people's children to help make ends meet. It beat crying myself to sleep and creating a stomach ulcer because of my guilt for sending my children to a sitter where they were not happy.

I beat myself up, crying myself to sleep and creating a stomach ulcer because of my guilt for sending my children to a sitter where they were not happy.

There is a line in the song that brings me to why I share this bit of me with you, my dear young one, "...I wish someone had a talked to me like I wanna talk to you."

You are more than you think you are. You just might not have met the people yet who will show you that. Believe me when I tell you, there is a great life out there for you, you can create it. I was blessed to meet a woman shortly after listening to the above song, and again I found myself quitting my job to be with my children. The planets aligned, and I was asked if I wanted to work for six months to cover maternity leave. It was shift work, and I did not need as much childcare with the kids in school and my husband at home at night. At that job, I met a woman who convinced me I was smart and that if I went and wrote the entrance exam for a University, I would pass it. The rest is history. That was the beginning of my becoming the person I was meant to be.

Please believe me when I say trust who you are and be you fully! The not so smart person I thought I was has gone to university and studied in Italy and Greece. I am a writer... yes even though I failed reading in grade 5, I am proud to be a published writer. I had a great, very unconventional career. Now I have the freedom to travel after retirement and continue that career by traveling across Canada and doing relief work when full-time staff takes holidays. Was it easy? No! Were there plenty of tears along the way? Yes! Would I do it again? You bet I would! Traveling to places worldwide, studying with excellent teachers, and meeting wonderfully supportive people is part of the life I have created. You have the power to do that, as well. I give you complete permission to spread your wings and fly!

Your Older Self!

Love Will Heal Us All

by Michelle Montero

My Love,

Life can come at you from different angles. In my experience, I wasn't always in control. My life used to be a complete nightmare. If I told you what happened to me, you'd think I was making it up, somehow *always* at the wrong place at the wrong time. I've dealt with mental health struggles, trauma from numerous sexual assaults, and homelessness!

I used to be so **bitter** and **angry**; I pushed away from the people who cared most about me and who only tried to help. I realized *I caused it all*. I was functioning on a negative frequency, always watching horror movies on Lifetime and viewing the news about people being kidnapped, raped, tortured, and murdered.

But finally, I unplugged the cord.

I shifted. I became selfish and picky. Refused to indulge in fear, anxiety, sadness, anger in my heart. I replaced my risky behaviors of drugs, alcohol, and dangerous promiscuity with self-love. I filled up that gaping hole in my heart with **every last shred** of love I had left in me.

It wasn't much at first.

Eventually, though it flourished into an *unwavering* and *fierce* desire to **love me and do all for myself** that I hadn't done yet. I learned to love every part of me that I hated and make love to me like **no one** ever could. I learned to *live* again.

Life's funny like that! It's a game - a playground. That thing that keeps happening to you is not without reason. You'll be in that loop until you *learn to surrender to yourself.* Stop resisting! Control what you **can** and *let the rest flow* like a river.

There is so much *beauty* and *room for creation* in those moments where you may feel **dread** but instead, walk past your dread –– **choose to let go instead...**

Trust the Universe to take care of you. She always has a way of making things fall into place at the perfectly *exact* moment. She loves you, and she won't let you fall. She's our everlasting, nurturing and loving mother who will always be there to catch you, my love.

Last year, I was about to become homeless, and in faith I simply stepped into surrender. I was **scared out of my mind** at first. But, eventually, I started to learn how to read Her little messages.

Have you ever had a need or desire for something, and somehow, it seemed to *magically* or coincidentally appear?

Except it wasn't a coincidence, my love.

Mother Universe speaks to us in a different language. Sometimes through nature or occurrences - **even through people who carry messages for us.** She's always *right* here with you. For you.

Whatever has you anxious, scared, feeling like giving up -- take a BIG, deep breath -- as big as you can. Now, with a smooth exhale, *release all of that tension and worry.* This is your message that everything's going to be okay. Things are going to *turn around,* and you are *going to make it!*

You are divinely:
- Gifted
- Guided
- Guarded
- Healthy
- Abundant

Mother Universe loves you so much, and so do I, sweet soul.

Be blessed, darling.

Your Older Self!

Celebrate Life with Laughter

by Mary Ananda Shakti

My Gorgeous Girl

Mary, you are loved more than you will ever know. You may have felt abandoned, unloved, and alone for a lot of the time but believe me, that was not the reality. You were never alone; your angels were always with you taking care of you. Your mam and dad had their hands full with you and your four siblings. They weren't able to give you all the attention you would have liked and needed. When bedtime came, they were exhausted. Then they would rise and do it all again the next day.

When you had your children, you were able to connect with these feelings and emotions. You realized how much your parents actually loved and cared for you, how much energy, responsibility, and commitment it took to raise children. They loved your children so much.

There was an outpouring of love for them always. Their grandchildren meant so much to them. Their lives were complete; their hearts fully open when they had the children around them.

So, dearest Mary, don't have any regrets about anything because you always did the best you could as a child. Then as an adult, as a daughter, then as a mother yourself. No one ever expected you to be perfect or to do things perfectly. Do live and express yourself in a more natural way that feels calm to you.

You don't need to be serious because everyone loves you and wishes only the best for you. Laugh and let go more. Play, dance, and sing. Be silly if you want to be. Express yourself fully through childlike playfulness. Get a degree if you desire; it will open more doors for you. Take care of your health, don't smoke, and go easy on the alcohol if you must drink. Go easy on the sweet stuff as well.

Be consistent and focused, know what you want, and focus on being a master of what you know and love.

Most of all, be loving, kind, and compassionate towards all living beings. Treasure your family and friends. Always love and respect your parents and give them plenty of hugs.

You must remember to have lots of fun and make beautiful memories for your future. Don't worry about the little things; Your life is for living fully in the present.

Oh! And get a dog when you can. Don't be afraid to let your hair go grey. Live by the sea. Routines help too, but not strict ones; be flexible.

Be an inspiration for others; encourage them to speak out as you do. Speak your truth; don't take things personally. Be a good friend, go the extra mile for others. Show and tell your children you love them. Be generous, and also save some money regularly. Never stop learning, challenge yourself. Make informed choices and never be afraid to be spontaneous.

Live and laugh out loud and do celebrate big because you deserve it. You are the purest of love.

Your Older Self!

Inner Guidance Leads to Healing

by Judith Richardson Schroeder

Oh, My Precious One,

It's been a long road, dear heart, from where you have been to where you now find yourself. The journey has been filled with peaks and valleys. Still, through it all, you have persisted -- envisioning a tomorrow that doesn't depend upon human-made cocktails of various chemically-based substitutes or stand-ins for those things your body has been unable to supply for many years.

You've always held fast to your belief that we are capable, as Spiritual beings, of the powerful gift of self-healing. Yet, you fought for so many years against your thoughts. That ran against your inner knowing. Instead, you fought against Doctors to avoid at all costs from ingesting medications designed to assist you yet seen by you as an unnecessary evil.

Your body fought against the human-made chemical cocktails as well. The side effects listed often as "rare" seemed always to find you, plague you, and deliver you the rarest ones listed!

I recall one situation in particular. The first time we faced suicidal thoughts together, you were fighting with a vengeance against the side-effects of a medication a Doctor at the time insisted could not possibly be happening. Yet, who could explain that day so long ago when we woke and spent several hours sitting on the kitchen floor planning, strategically and meticulously, our demise?

By 2:30 that afternoon, a plan that would leave us

free from pain, brain fog, the horrific struggle that was now our life after a very slight car accident a few months earlier. We would drift off to sleep peacefully. As we picked ourselves up off the kitchen floor, a booming voice echoed in our ear!

"JUDY!" It was forceful, deep baritone, powerfully commanding. It brought us out of our numbness, our planning, our disassociated state, and allowed us the blessing to realize this was NOT supposed to be.

It wouldn't be. And, when we called the Doctor, and he realized we were NOT joking? We were not making this up? It was NOT all in our head? Finally, he listened!

Human-made medications would be something our body would fight against for years to come.

Although medicines today have and continue to help millions of people worldwide, there is a tiny percentage of the population, less than 10%, whose bodies react poorly to even a single ingredient, and you, dear heart are one of those people.

This journey has brought you to the other side of

living with a chronic illness. For you, there has been a gift of "seeing" and insight that your body, Spirit, Soul, and Mind have led you to. Every natural solution you have explored has been delivered to you through unique and serendipitous means, and for you, worth the exploration.

Worth the research. Worth the effort to investigate.

You have been medication-free for seven years now!

You have, through various modalities, teachings, efforts, and protocols, naturally aligned to your body, mind, and soul's challenges and found a place where life is always and forever a blessing every single day. Where pain is no longer the yardstick by which you measure the quality of your life.

This healing path has been one that has also allowed us to have a deep, beautiful connection to our mind and heart, trusting in our instinctual wisdom as we listen to our intuitive self.

Thank you, young one, for your immense courage, stamina, instinctual intuitiveness, and for having the heart to step through the battle with tremendous purpose and vision. I am eternally grateful. x

Your Older Self!

Little You

by Tanisha Chambers

Dear Younger Self,

Little you don't cry,

Tears of joy and sadness mixed up in one,

Tears dripping down, forming puddles.

Little you don't cry,

I will take care of you,

You are a special one.

As I dry my tears and calm my heart,

I remember to forgive myself for all is not right.

I remember that life is a learning experience,

And all things will be alright.

Little you remember you are meant for greatness.

And nothing is easy!

Little you, don't cry,

Some parts are rocky,

Some a little steady.

But trust the process for you, little you.

Will always be enough.

As I look back on imagining the young, frail me and writing this chapter to my younger self, it's a little difficult. There is so much that I need to say to myself, and I don't know where to start. Do I write Dear Tanisha? Perhaps the perfect place to start is by telling the younger me that I forgive you for all of your decisions in life. All great starting points; however, the poem brings the right calmness and sums up some of what I needed to say. So, I decided to do something different and introduce a poem that my younger self feels, even in my adult life. I still experience those same tears, and I feel that same pain. Even though I believe it, I now understand that I am no longer in that space; I now know and have overcome my past hurt, and honestly, I believe that my journey is what I was supposed to experience. My journey shaped me into the woman that I am today. So, I feel ok; it's important not to stay in the past, instead, it is better to learn, and grow and share, and teach my experience to others that they may have a point of reference to leap from.

Over the years, I have learned so much from my mom. Although she did not know everything, she did do her best. I took her experience of what I could remember. Is that not the point of life? to learn from your parent's wrongs and try and do better? When we are younger, we are taught to follow and behave in a certain way, and our upbringing has shaped many of us, but the point is to grow. Who and how I was then, and how I was raised should not define me, and it should be my duty as I grow, to experience and learn new things about life to also strive to do better. That is what I have done. I never blamed my parents, teachers, family members, society for my struggles. For yes, all of these people have shaped me. Over the years, I have learned to unlearn some of my teachings and search for greater purpose and understanding even though this did not come easy to me, I realized I had to change my paradigms as I grew.

Younger me, I love you, always and forever! You have been my rock; you have always had big dreams and aspired to do more. I can see that you were a natural star, even if you did not see it. Although you have sacrificed a lot for your family, and you have always put family first, you never complained. You knew and felt great comfort and happiness in being the giving and loving person you are. I am sorry that it may have not always been appreciated, or that your rights sometimes came off as wrong. I know you did your best through the years, and although at times, you were discouraged you bravely kept pushing. I wonder why you didn't give you more credit.

Perhaps now you can.

Your Older Self!

Stream of consciousness: wisdom that transcends past, present, and future

by Dr. Malaika Katrina Singleton

Dear Younger Self,

Follow your bliss. What is it that makes you happy? Take time to ponder this question. Once you find it, do it as often as you can. Don't let life get in the way of that bliss. Make time!

Know thyself. Know your history and history in general. It will help to make sense of the world. Study religion to understand human psychology, sociology, and world views, but cultivate your own sense of spiritual understanding. Keep an open, curious mind. Remember that you control how you see yourself and feel about yourself, not others. Nothing external defines you.

Do what's right for you. Put yourself first. Save, save, save, and invest in things you have educated yourself on. Take risks. Be open to making mistakes. Learn from them, but never quit. Pursue your wildest dreams and your loftiest goals. You've got that time ahead of you anyway. Stand up and stand firm for yourself, your rights, and for the rights of others. Tell the truth. Speak the truth, no matter how unpleasant, because the truth will always matter.

Love yourself. Cultivate yourself. Indulge yourself. Take care of yourself.

Learn to be your own best friend and keep yourself company. This relationship sets the tone and quality for all others yet to follow.

It's okay to rest. It's okay to do nothing. It's okay to set boundaries. It's okay simply to want peace, quiet, and tranquility and not want to be bothered sometimes. There is personal power in claiming your space and solitude. To want to go your chosen way and to want to do things differently than the norm. It's okay to say no, to decline, without explanation. It is respecting you.

It's okay to protect your peace, to sever cords and connections, to start over again and again. It's okay to be human and feel and express the full gamut of emotions that lie within you. It's okay to let go and to move on.

Travel as often as you can. You never know what can happen in life, do it while you are young, healthy, and during a time when you may have little to no obligations. Maintain your sense of self and self-worth no matter what's going on around you. Remember who you are and where you came from to be here. Remember also, just how far you've come! Celebrate that! Know that you can begin again — any time.

Listen to your intuition. Heed the whispers and nudges of your ancestors. The rustling of their stories as the wind passes among the trees. There is a generosity of wisdom that can be born from stillness.

Know that you are the creator with every thought, word, feeling, and deed that passes in and out of your awareness. You can always affect change by speaking up and, if need be, acting out to raise awareness, educate, inform, engage, and inspire.

Your Older Self!

A Final Message

"I raise up my voice---not so I can shout but so that those without a voice can be heard."

~Malala Yousafzai

Imagine if we all shared our authentic voice and our messages with the world? There is nothing stopping you. Now that you have read all the messages shared here, it is time for you to embark on your own journey of creating your message to your younger self. We encourage you to reflect on your life and think about what are some of the life changing lessons that you have learned so far in your journey. Journal your thoughts and use these as your own personal reminders to uplift you and those around you. There is nothing more powerful than seeing a woman speaking her truth and encouraging us all to rise together.

There has never been a more critical time in our history to make a difference and that difference comes from us all contributing and sharing our stories and our lessons with those who are also on a similar journey, even if they are one step behind. It is our hope that from reading the messages within this book that you too will create your own ripple, it only takes one small act to begin.

We would love to know what you think of the book, so please share with us at info@ carnelianmoonpublishing.com.

About The Publishers

Carnelian Moon Publishing, Inc., is a hybrid publishing service for heart-centered female authors who are ready to birth their first or next book. We believe that the authoring journey is more than writing a book, because authors are taken on a transformational journey as they write each word, it provides healing from deep within.

By working in partnership with you to provide a memorable and inspiring VIPXperience as you breathe life into your book, Carnelian Moon Publishing is with you every step of your journey from idea through to over 40,000 distribution outlets worldwide.

For discerning authors seeking a truly collaborative publishing experience, Carnelian Moon Publishing's team of professionals deliver support, guidance, service, and knowledge which encourages new, seasoned and serial authors the confidence to dedicate their time and attention to there craft, knowing the publishing details are well in hand.

With a defined Mission to provide guidance to 1000 best-selling authors in 5 years, infusing the world with empowerment, inspiration, leadership, passion, purpose, healing, and love, authors are finding the fresh approach Carnelian Moon Publishing along with their Imprints for Children's authors, male & female authors, and Metaphysical authors delivers, to be a perfect fit no matter where the author is on their journey.

Carnelian Moon Publishing takes away the overwhelm and challenges too long associated with publishing and inherently believes your authoring journey is meant to be a blissful one from your heart to readers worldwide. Their team of experts are ready to assist you in making your authoring experience an easeful, streamlined, organized, and personalized experience at every step. Whether you choose to self-publish or prefer to dedicate your focus to writing leaving the details to others, Carnelian Moon Publishing has the solution that is perfect for you and your vision, goals, and authoring success!

The founding corner stones Carnelian Moon Publishing adheres to ensures every step taken is in alignment with you the author and adheres to the Agency's core values:

- Authenticity & Truth
- Value & Reliability
- Community & Support
- Clarity & Focus

When the self-publishing author, children's author, personal development, or Spiritually-based author in you yearns to share your wisdom with the world, Carnelian Moon Publishing, Inc., is ready to welcome you to the Carnelian Moon family of exceptional authors.

Find out more about us at *carnelianmoonpublishing. com.*

About Our Authors

Mary Ananda Shakti

Mary is a Life and Laughter Coach with over 25 years' experience of deep inner work and healing. She is also a Shamanic Coach and shape shifter. She supports people in awakening their fountain of Bliss within so they too can live their most phenomenal life. Connect with Mary:

Connect with Mary:
Website: laughteryogaireland.org
Email: maryanandashakti@gmail.com

Allistar Banks

Allistar Banks was born and raised in McCormick South Carolina. Ms. Banks is a graduate of Lander University in Greenwood, SC and received her Bachelor's Degree in Mass Communications. At the age of eight, she discovered her passion for writing children's books. Ms. Banks focuses on creating stories that are fun and educational. Also, her blog focuses on stories that are based on her experiences and also lessons for children to learn. The Author has been featured in the Index Journal, Press & Banner, McCormick Messenger, and in Lander University's magazine for her children's books.

Connect with Allistar:

Website: allistartheauthor.com

Debbie Belnavis-Brimble

Debbie was born in England and spent most of her childhood in Jamaica where she developed a passion for supporting others in need. She has focused the last 12 years of her life supporting women through her coaching and mentoring programs through the Inner Brilliance Academy. More recently she started two organisations to support women share their messages and stories through books, podcasts and events. She is also a #1 International Best-Selling Author of several books.

Connect with Debbie:
Websites: Coaching & Mentoring:
innerbrillianceacademy.com
Publishing: carnelianmoonpublishing.com
Share Your Message: behindthoseheels.com

Donna Brown

Donna Brown is a strategist and speaker. She helps visionaries design and scale brands that impact millions. Known for her understanding of trends, she leads leaders to a new, deeper understanding and application of the purpose and practice of business. With decades of experience in design, media, entrepreneurship and digital marketing, Donna is a multi-faceted innovative solution-finder and anchor for her clients.

Connect with Donna:

Website: donnabrown.com

Tanisha Campbell

Tanisha was born and raised in Philly to Jamaican parents. She graduated from Martin Luther King High school and later graduated from Rosemont College. During her time in college she wrote many stories and poetry for her Women's Studies classes that brought back memories of her reading and writing as a child.

Tanisha currently has four book out Zuri and the Monster, Zuri and the monster coloring book, Zuri's Day of Pranks and her latest books Beauty Defined by Me, which is also part of the Zuri series. Tanisha hopes to bring back the tradition of parents and kids taking the time out to read and enjoy the small things in life.

Connect with Tanisha:
Website: tanishachambers.com

Jean Day

Jean Day is from a small town in Georgia. She holds a bachelor's degree from Mount St. Mary's University and a master's degree from Pepperdine University in Los Angeles.

She has worked both in private practice as a mental health practitioner and as a college instructor at Georgia Highlands College. Jean has twenty-three years of experience in the field of psychology.

She is a co-author, radio personality and also co-hosts a podcast called Fun, Feisty, Fabulous for women over 40. Jean resides in Georgia and loves traveling around the US.

She also volunteers as a mentor at Cartersville City Schools and the Salvation Army.

Carra Dixon

Carra is a 34-year-old woman from Philadelphia PA. She grew up with many adversities from abuse, neglect, drugs, alcohol and mental illness. She was silenced as a young girl. Her mother had it hard and her father was in prison most of her life. She was raised by her grandmother for the most impressionable years of her life, who taught her confidence, pride, and strength amongst other things as a young black girl. She fell in love with writing as a way to express herself. She loves to journal, story tell, and writing poetry. She just finished her first published book, *Mommy is not God* and is a part of two anthology books. She hopes that her writing will help to heal others.

Konyka Dunson

Konyka Dunson, an inspirational speaker, award-winning television host and transformational workshop leader, is the author of the forthcoming book, "Sacred and Overflowing: A 30 Day Devotion to the Woman God Called You to Be." Konyka's mission, with every audience, is always a breakthrough—to move forward on the highest possibilities.

Connect with Konyka:
Website: KonykaDunson.com
Facebook: @Konykatv
Twitter: @kdsoul

Cassie Ferrer

Cassie Ferrer is an Award-Winning financial leader. She is a Money Coach helping families to live the debt free lifestyle and teaching investment strategies that lead to a legacy of wealth. She is speaker, an Amazon best-selling author, Host of Behind those Heels Podcast, and Founder of Behind those Heels and Numbers Nerd Consulting, LLC.

Connect with Cassie:
Behind those Heels:
Website: : behindthoseheels.com
Facebook: facebook.com/behindthoseheels

Numbers Nerd Consulting:
Website: numbersnerdconsulting.com
Facebook: Numbers-Nerd-Consulting-1002141682 93931

Cathy Gagliardi

Cathy Gagliardi currently enjoys being surrounded at her home with her mom close by, enjoying the beauty of nature near Hamilton, Ontario, Canada. Her sons, Patrick and Gregory, encourage her dreams big!

Cathy is the author of several books helping children deal with anxiety and develop compassion for others while learning to accept themselves.

Connect with Cathy:
Website: twinklinglynx.com
Facebook: TwinklingLynx-2479264172118444

Nikita McKenzie

Inspiring, encouraging, confident, powerful, resilient, trustworthy, empowered ... IAmShe Nikita is her brand! A woman with a strong commitment to becoming everything that God intended, IAmShe Nikita made a decision to choose faith over fear.

With a compassionate heart to help women confidently pursue purpose and maximize their potential, her vision finally met her purpose! IAmShe Nikita is the founder of I Am Someone He Empowered, INC., a nonprofit organization established to support women as they transition through the many obstacles that come to shape their definition of themselves.

Michelle Montero

Michelle wears many different hats! She is a digital marketing strategist, author, cat and dog mommy and soon to be a first-time mom. She had her first taste of writing when she shared her story in *Behind Those Heels: Eleven Powerful Messages to Inspire and Ignite Change*. She is honored to use her presence as a way to spread her message for love, happiness, justice and equality for everyone.

Michelle helps coaches and healers establish a strong online presence by using digital marketing strategy and design.

Connect with Michelle:
Website: michellemontero.us
Facebook: @MichelleMonteroMarketing
Instagram: @MichelleMonteroMarketing

Sara Olson

Sara is an Empowerment Coach, author, and artist with 20 years of leadership experience. Sara has been featured in Forbes Magazine representing a previous company she worked for. It is Sara's goal to utilize her books, art, and businesses to establish a Non-profit organization for Single Parents. Sara is currently writing a book about her own story which shares her journey as a single parent. She believes that things happen for us, not to us, we are never too old, young, fat, skinny, or (whatever excuse to fill in the blank) to make a difference in your family, community, and ultimately the world and to rewrite your story to have that *"Happy Ending"* and make your dreams of reality.

Connect with Sara:

Website: mycouageousmasterpiece.com

Judith Richardson Schroeder

Judith is a Sub-conscious Behaviorist, Master Hypnotist, Life Purpose Coach, and Best-Selling Author. She is a Co-founding partner and Publisher with the uniquely Hybrid Publishing House, Carnelian Moon Publishing, Inc.

When not assisting authors to achieve their publishing visions, Judith assists clients to uncover their inner gifts, encouraging them to explore their own personal mind map to uncover and remove blockages that keep them from living a life rich in true gratitude, fulfillment, and success.

When not helping others, she enjoys speaking through her art and photography. Her favorite pastimes are traveling with her husband and spending time with her beautiful granddaughters Arya and Lyla, and her own children.

Chrisa Riviello

Chrisa Riviello is a psychic medium with the compassion and talents to provide her clients with an exceptional experience that may very well change their lives.

Chrisa has been on a spiritual journey for some time and after the gift of courage to accept her role it has been amazing to be a true guardian to help others to overcome obstacles and gain a sense of peace.

Chrisa lives in Mullica Hill, NJ.

Connect with Chrisa:
Website: mullicahillmedium.com
Facebook: facebook.com/MullicaHillMedium

Dr. Malaika Singleton

Dr. Malaika Singleton is a science policy expert, author, non-profit executive, serial entrepreneur, and freelance copy editor.

She holds a bachelor's degree in biology and psychology, jointly awarded by Rutgers University-Newark College of Arts and Sciences/ New Jersey Institute of Technology, and a doctorate in neuroscience from the University of California, Davis.

Connect with Dr. Malaika:
Website: saintniafoundation.org
Website: theproofdocs.com

Cindy Winsor

Cindy Winsor is a single mother of three. She can usually be found outside in her gardens, talking to her flowers, or in her workshop, creating something, be it jewelry, blankets, food or furniture. Living in a small Ontario, Canada town, she is learning daily to love herself a little more, and to receive her raindrops.

Janet Wiszowaty

Janet retired from a Career in the Royal Canadian Mounted Police as an Emergency Police Dispatcher in 2011. After being diagnosed with Post Traumatic Stress Disorder in 2003, Janet went on a journey of discovery through Personal Development where she trained and was certified in Jack Canfield's Success Principles, Marcia Wieder's Dream Coaching and Neuro-Linguistic Programming, Hypnotherapy and Time-Line Therapy tm. She uses all the tools to help others move forward from their trauma or "Now What" stage to keep moving forward toward their dreams.

Connect with Janet:
Facebook: facebook.com/YourNowWhatCoach
Instagram: NowWhatCoach@WorldlyConnekts
Email: janet.wiszowaty@gmail.com

CPSIA information can be obtained
at www.ICGtesting.com
Printed in the USA
FSHW011823250121
77944FS